GOD'S TRUE INTENT

AND PURPOSE

FOR HUMANITY

By

Paul Dalton

Table of Contents

Acknowledgments

My publisher asked me if I wanted to acknowledge someone, or persons, who had made an impact on my life and the creation of this book. I remembered an aunt and uncle who never gave up on me, an old cowboy whose code of life I took to heart as a young boy, and different pastors who had, and some who still do, have the courage to teach with boldness without regret.

I thought of all the times I should have died and yet lived. My first near death experience I stumbled onto as a five year old when I catapulted out of a speeding car on a freeway. The next similar experience that I vividly recall was when I fell into a fast spring-filled river. At the precise spot, my uncle reached out and, at the last second, grabbed my shirt and snatched me from the jaws of the murderous current. My skin still feels the heat of the inferno while serving in a platoon of 25 men in Vietnam. We were surrounded by NVA soldiers in a Hollywood like firefight and the only thought that engulfed me was, "this is it." During all of this, I felt a gentle nudge, heard a silent whisper signaling me to remain calm. I am safe. How can I forget my physical incarceration inside the walls of prison? Life could be bought or sold for a cup of coffee. It dawned on me that all through my life there had always been one true "best friend" who had stood with me, at my side, never failing, and always there. It was the Lord God Almighty! Father, Son and Spirit, always watching over me, even when I was defiant. Knowing that a day would come when, in utter humbleness, I would surrender my whole heart and life to Them.

They are the Ones to whom I owe my existence and life. They have placed these words, written in this book, on my heart to share in times such as these we live in today. I am nothing, but They are everything. I can only acknowledge the One True Living God who rules the vast universe we live in.

Dedication

I would like to thank all those whose encouragement and prayers have been a true blessing to me. Those who helped print this book so it was able to be in the hands of thousands of people. You all remain in my prayers and that the Father of our Lord Jesus Christ will bless you all.

This book could never have happened without the patience, kindness, willingness to listen and the love of my wife, Linda Sue Dalton, who never failed me.

About the Author

Paul Dalton was raised in a dysfunctional family. Hence, for him, anywhere was always a better place to be than his home. Circumstances compelled him to mature, earlier as he had to provide for himself at the age of thirteen.

The author lived in many states across America, giving him a perspective of different races and cultures that he will always value. Once, he visited a church in Charleston, South Carolina, he recalled, "What a wonderful time I had!" Being invited to have lunch with a family and learning from a wise man that God loves everyone regardless of who they are or their appearance, elevated his experience.

When Paul Dalton turned 18 he found himself in Vietnam with the 173rd Airborne Brigade. It was 1968 – a time the author came to love and hate. He understood the true meaning of brotherhood, and that family is not always by blood. He observed and experienced things that no 18-year-old should endure. Being confined and recovering in a hospital in Japan allowed Dalton to reflect on what he had experienced and endured.

As he came back from the war, the nation welcomed him with contempt. Suffering the loss of soldier brothers plunged Dalton's world into dissonance. Understanding the truth of the war, the lies of the nation that its young men had been told, threw Dalton down a dark path of violence, drugs and ultimately prison. He considers this journey as regretful even today.

It is only by the grace of God, the loving sacrifice of His Son, and His mercy, that Dalton was able to turn his life around and find the peace in his soul he had always sought but never found until recently. The last time he saw his father was when he was 12 years old. His last words were, "Don't be a fence sitter. Make a decision, right or wrong. Learn from your choices."

Life is all or nothing, we can't live our lives halfway.

"So who am I?" the author asks himself.

"A simple, humble man, joined together with a loving wife as One, whose lifelong journey has finally brought him home at last."

Introduction

I was blessed by people in my life that taught me to "think," to question and to not accept things at their face value. My college professor, in his opening statement of our philosophy class was, to the effect, if you leave my class with more questions than answers I will have done my job well.

Many years ago, I sought the true meaning of life. The question, "What is the truth?" Is God and His Son real? Is the Bible in fact true and trustworthy? Was this theory of Evolution true or fiction? I spent time learning Eastern Philosophy. I spent time studying under the teachings of a renowned Eastern/Indian Philosopher who led me to the Taoist teachings. In studying the Tao Te Ching I found a common ground with Christianity in that the Taoist believe that this physical body is not our true self; that we are spiritual beings, and that when the body dies the "spirit" lives on. Through these times of searching, I really never found the "truth" or the peace that comes through it that I was really searching for.

Upon the birth of my son, I elected to go to a Christian church. I knew the life I was living was not that type of life I wanted for my son to witness. I still looked for inspiration that would prove to me the "truth" of this world we live in. I found it in a tiny church in Warrenton, Oregon with about 30 people that had a young pastor named Jason Biel. He had a unique method of teaching. He taught the Bible verse-by-verse, book-by-book. He taught the length, breadth, and depth of God's word in its fullness. His desire to share the "full gospel" instead of a "light" overview was a blessing I will always cherish. Through Jason's faithfulness this little church grew to hundreds of people and a large facility. During this time, I came across a man named Chuck Missler. His understanding of the Bible and the history of mankind amazed me. I wrote him and his wife Nancy a letter. One day, while getting ready to get a haircut, I received a phone call from Nancy Missler. It was a call that changed my life greatly. I would like to thank Chuck and Nancy Missler for proving to me the authenticity of the Bible and that the Bible spoke of history far in advance of its time. That only God, who exists outside of time and space, could have given the words of prophecy, the future events of history, hundreds of years before they would take place.

Though I had good teachers and a foundation for the real truth that was being laid, there were still trials in my life, changes in my life God needed to accomplish in me, that I had to go through, learn from and remove the desires of myself in order for God and His Son to bring me to where I am today. As you read, I trust you will come to understand that, whether or not we like to admit it, we all are being shaped and molded by the world we live in, the things we accept and believe in. This is our "proving ground" for God's Kingdom and all eternity.

Understanding that everything God does has Intent and Purpose. His ability to see the beginning and ending of time allows Him to orchestrate a plan, a series of events that allows Him to reach His desired goal or end. So, I questioned, "What is God's plan for humanity?" What is His Intent and Purpose? This is what this book is about. His Plan,

His goal and desire for those who live on this Earth. I believe that God and His Son has placed this task in my heart and I hope those of you who read this book can find the understanding, wisdom, and peace from knowing that They, Father and Son, had a plan for all who have ever lived on Earth. In the book of *Galatians 1:3-5* we read, *"Grace to you and peace from God the Father and our Lord Jesus Christ, who gave Himself for our sins, that He might deliver us from this present evil age, according to the will of our God and Father, to whom be glory forever and ever. Amen."*

We live in this "evil age" according to Paul's letter to the Galatians and all of this is "according to the will of our God and Father." This is all according to His will, and His Intent, and Purpose. The age we all live in holds a unique purpose for all humanity and if you allow the Holy Spirit to remove the blindness of this world you will see and understand the true Will, Intent, and Purpose of our Heavenly Father.

Chapter 1: The Question

I have often wondered why, in God's wisdom and knowledge of all things, that He would place the Tree of the Knowledge of Good and Evil in the Garden of Eden in the very beginning. We know that God lives outside of time. He can see in advance, events, courses of history, the future of individual lives, and yet He elected to place one tree in which man could not eat from in the Garden. Why did God do this? I believe that this is one of the greatest mysteries.

There is no evidence in the Bible that God, or His Son, have ever done anything by happenstance. There has always been Intent and Purpose in everything They have ever done. The outcome of Their actions was also known to Them in advance. Therefore, if God knew Eve would be deceived by Satan, and Adam would willingly sin, why allow Satan the ability to corrupt humanity and all that had been created? The Father and the Son had to see all the events that would take place on Earth once They permitted Satan to create sin on Earth. They had to know all the horror that humanity would inflict upon itself. The wars, the Holocaust of WWII, human greed and all its effects in the world. The evil done every day of human existence to little children who are the most innocent of all of us. God knew there would be human suffering beyond measure. His Son knew everything we see each day, or written in books of human history, and all that will happen tomorrow, will take place. Yes, They knew and have allowed all that has happened these past thousands of years. The pain, suffering, and blood shed that has taken place had to be allowed by the Father for a reason. For a purpose, and if so "what" and "why?"

It's natural to think that since God is good, why is there so much pain and suffering in the world? That is a question I have asked for many years. As you read this book I trust you will see the truth in God's plan for all humanity. This world is nothing but a test from God. He tests our patience, perseverance, honesty, and our overall character by placing us in various situations. Sometimes, He will test you by blessing you with a reward, and other times, He will test you by traversing you through a hard trial.

These following verses show us the Father's intent, *"The Lord tests the righteous, But the wicked and the one who loves violence His soul hates." Psalms 11:5.* In *James 1:12* we read, *"Blessed is the man who endures temptation; for when he has been approved, he will receive the crown of life which the Lord has promised to those who love Him."*

The aforementioned verses indicate God's promise to reward those for their trials and tribulations, and most importantly their LOVE for Him. When suffering is endured for the sake of knowing and loving the Lord Jesus Christ, the afflicted person earns himself rewards in heaven. Moses spoke of Israel's testing in *Exodus 20:20, "And Moses said to the people, "Do not fear; for God has come to test you, and that His fear may be before you, so that you may not sin."* Trusting God in difficult times and remembering Him in good times will always keep us closer to Him and prevent us from committing sin.

The attitude we must all acquire to live our day-to-day lives is narrated through the following verses:

"Examine me, O Lord, and prove me; Try my mind and heart."
Psalms 26:2

"Search me, O God, and know my heart; Try me, and know my anxieties; And see if there is any wicked way in me, And lead me in the way everlasting." Psalms 139:23-24

"Examine yourselves as to whether you are in the faith. Test yourselves. Do you not know yourselves, that Jesus Christ is in you? – unless indeed you are disqualified." 2 Corinthians 13:5

"Test all things; hold fast what is good." 1 Thessalonians 5:21

Chapter 2- The Beginning

The transformation of Lucifer, an Arc Angel of beauty, to Satan and the realm of darkness was the beginning. We learn in *Revelation 12:7-9* that there was a great war in Heaven between God and Satan. There is not much said about the events of the actual war itself. Satan and one-third of the angels were removed from Heaven and cast out. Our books on the history of wars are numerous. They provide details of each war. This allows students of war to study and learn from the errors of past leadership. The Bible is absent of details of this war in Heaven. We have all read what an angry God can do to those on this Earth when they defy Him. I am sure Egypt's Pharaoh would have taken better swimming lessons or Sodom and Gomorrah probably would have repented rather than see such fire come down from Heaven and destroy their very existence. Many have looked upon the planets in our universe and questioned if some of the things we see are the result of such a war. We read in *1 John 3:8*, *"He who sins is of the devil, for the devil has sinned from the beginning. For this purpose the Son of God was manifested, that He might destroy the works of the devil."* We learn from this passage when sin entered into God's Kingdom and a purpose for His Son to deal with Satan and sin.

This was the beginning that has given birth to all we have read and seen of Earth's history and experienced in each of our lives. We have lived with the effects of sin, failing bodies ravaged by diseases, evil acts we carry out upon one another, merciless wars, greed and prideful self-righteousness. When we read *Ezekiel 28*, we find a description of Lucifer before he sinned. He was an anointed Cherub, he was perfect in his way and his beauty was magnificent. His voice must have been beyond measure as we read in *Verse 13, "...The workmanship of your timbrels and pipes was prepared for you on the day you were created."* The detailed verse of Lucifer can be found in *Ezekiel 28:12-15, "Son of man, take up a lamentation for the king of Tyre, and say to him, "Thus says the Lord God:*

"You were the seal of perfection,
Full of wisdom and perfect in beauty.
You were in Eden, the garden of God;
Every precious stone was your covering:
The sardius, topaz, and diamond,
Beryl, onyx, and jasper,
Sapphire, turquoise, and emerald with gold.
The workmanship of your timbrels and pipes
Was prepared for you on the day you were created.
You were the anointed cherub who covers;
I established you;
You were on the holy mountain of God;
You walked back and forth in the midst of fiery stones.
You were perfect in your ways from the day you were created,
Till iniquity was found in you."

We also see that Lucifer was in the Garden of Eden. Most Bible scholars will agree that it was Jesus who was the actual creator of this Earth. In *Ephesians 3:9* we read, *"...God, who created all things through Jesus Christ;..."* Also in *Colossians 1:15-17* we read, *"He is the image of the invisible God, the firstborn over all creation. For by Him all things were created that are in heaven and that are on earth, visible and invisible, whether thrones or dominions or principalities or powers. All things were created through Him and for Him. And He is before all things, and in Him all things consist."*

1 Corinthians 8:6, "yet for us there is one God, the Father, of whom are all things, and we for Him; and one Lord Jesus Christ, through whom are all things, and through whom we live."

John 1:10, "He was in the world, and the world was made through Him, and the world did not know Him." I have often wondered if Lucifer's jealousy was in fact against Jesus more so than the Father. Did Jesus, who was the Father's only begotten Son, make him jealous of His ability, through the power given to Him by the Father, to create Earth? We learn from *Isaiah 14:13-14, "For you have said in your heart: 'I will ascend into heaven, I will exalt my throne above the stars of God; I will also sit on the mount of the congregation On the farthest sides of the north; I will ascend above the heights of the clouds, I will be like the Most High."* Whatever caused Lucifer to change his heart, his own desire to be like God, other than his jealous rage, we will probably not fully understand until we are in Heaven. Maybe God will have a heavenly video tape of Lucifer's fall for us to see. Regardless, we all have come to understand that sin can never be allowed to exist if there is to be happiness as God intended for us to have. Lucifer's fall from grace is a lesson for all of humanity. Lucifer became so proud of his own power, position, beauty, and intelligence that he started to desire for greater honor, glory, and power, designated to God and His Son alone. Pride was the beginning of the deadly sin of pride in oneself. Lucifer became The Fallen Angel of Pride. Thus, pride should be avoided. As *Proverbs 11:2* says, *"When pride comes, then comes shame; But with the humble is wisdom."* To avoid being prideful, it's best to remain humble.

Chapter 3 – War Comes to Earth

We now find that Lucifer and one third of God's angels were cast out of Heaven. I have often wondered why God the Father did not just destroy Lucifer and his angels that rebelled. It would have been so easy for Him to do so. He is the Creator of all things. Is not the Father going to cast Satan and his angels into the lake of fire at the very end of this Earth's history? Yes, God will cast him, his angels, and all who refuse to love Him and His Son. Did all of Heaven need to see that the Father was right, His actions were justified and true? That someone like Satan and his darkness could never become anything but pure evil. You and I witness Satan's desire to destroy us and foil God's plan each day.

So where did the Father cast them to? *Revelation 12:9*, *"So the great dragon was cast out, that serpent of old, called the Devil and Satan, who deceives the whole world; he was cast to the earth, and his angels were cast out with him."* So now the stage is set. God's plan for humanity is about to begin.

In the Book of Genesis, we read that God made the Heavens and the Earth. He created all life and a beautiful Earth full of living creatures and beauty. The Holy Bible, in *Genesis 1:1* says, *"In the beginning God created the heavens and the earth."* In *Hebrews 1:10* we read, *"And: You, Lord, in the beginning laid the foundation of the earth, And the heavens are the work of Your hands."* In the Book of *Nehemiah*, *Chapter 9:6*, he wrote, *"You alone are the Lord; You have made heaven, The heaven of heavens, with all their hosts, The earth and everything* on it, The seas and all that is in them, And You preserve them all. The host of heaven worships You."

I have often contemplated the joy He had in creating all the beauty. The many colorful birds of the air, the wonderful colorful flowers, each animal and a perfect Earth for all to dwell in. I am sure He had much joy in doing so.

Genesis 1:20, "Then God said, "Let the waters abound with an abundance of living creatures, and let birds fly above the earth across the face of the firmament of the heavens."

Genesis 1:21, "So God created great sea creatures and every living thing that moves, with which the waters abounded, according to their kind, and every winged bird according to its kind. And God saw that it was good."

In *Genesis 1:22, "And God blessed them, saying, "Be fruitful and multiply, and fill the waters in the seas, and let birds multiply on the earth."*

God said in *Genesis 1:24, " Then God said, "Let the earth bring forth the living creature according to its kind: cattle and creeping thing and beast of the earth, each according to its kind"*; and it was so.

God also said in *Genesis 1:25, "And God made the beast of the earth according to its kind, cattle according to its kind, and everything that creeps on the earth according to its kind. And God saw that it was good."*

Genesis 1:27 we read, *"So God created man in His own image; in the image of God He created him; male and female He created them."* Adam and Eve were given charge of this Earth. They were caretakers of all that God had created. They were told to multiply, fill the Earth and subdue it. Adam walked with God in the cool of the day. Adam saw God face-to-face! Imagine that, walking with our Creator and having long conversations with Him. One day we all, who are saved, will see Jesus as He is because we are told we will be like Him. We shall be Sons and Daughters of the Most High God and His Son. What a joy that will be.

After Eve was created, we read in *Genesis 2:23*, *"And Adam said: "This is now bone of my bones And flesh of my flesh; She shall be called Woman Because she was taken out of Man."* We also read in *Verse 24*, *"Therefore a man shall leave his father and mother and be joined to his wife, and they shall become one flesh."*

As we read in Genesis, Satan came to destroy all that Jesus and His Father created. Satan is morally corrupt. His purpose is to entice us to sin. He inflicts disease and shatters those who are in the image of God and seduces us to commit crimes and grave errors. Satan is sly, wicked, and deceptive. He distracts believers from God's plan and leads their way into deception and lies, as evident in the following verses:

"Now the serpent was more cunning than any beast of the field which the Lord God had made. And he said to the woman, "Has God indeed said, 'You shall not eat of every tree of the garden?" And the woman said to the serpent, "We may eat the fruit of the trees of the garden; but of the fruit of the tree which is in the midst of the garden, God has said, 'You shall not eat it, nor shall you touch it, lest you die.' " Then the serpent said to the woman,

"You will not surely die. For God knows that in the day you eat of it your eyes will be opened, and you will be like God, knowing good and evil." Genesis 3:1-5. Satan's purpose is to deceive and misrepresent God. The Lord NEVER told Adam that he could not touch the Tree of the Knowledge of Good and Evil! Satan is still very cunning today and we can never let our guard down for one second.

Most scholars agree that Satan deceived Eve. Adam, of his own free will, elected to take a bite of the fruit of the Tree of Knowledge of Good and Evil, bringing about sin to this world and all of humanity. *1 Timothy 2:14* confirms this, *"And Adam was not deceived, but the woman being deceived, fell into transgression."* Why did Adam do so? Adam walked with God each day and had conversations with God. Adam also obtained wisdom and understanding from conversations with God. So why did he choose freely to create sin in the human race? The Bible does not tell us what his thinking was; or his reason to eat of the forbidden fruit. We will never know the truth till we reach Heaven. However, I have a personal belief which has given me some peace of why Adam took a bite of the forbidden fruit given to him by his wife.

The Bible tells us that the two became one flesh. Adam and Eve were made perfect in every way. They were a direct creation of God, and most likely, Jesus Himself. Adam had a "love" for Eve that you and I cannot begin to understand.

Adam was made perfect and so his love was perfect according to what God created in him. I can only ponder the type of love Adam had for Eve. They were, truly, direct creations of God. We read in *Genesis 2:7*, *"And the Lord God formed man of the dust of the ground, and breathed into his nostrils the breath of life; and man became a living being."* But God found that it was not good for man to be alone, so in *Genesis 2:18* we read, *"And the Lord God said, "It is not good that man should be alone; I will make him a helper comparable to him."* So, the Lord took a rib from Adam's body and created Eve.

After Eve ate from the forbidden fruit, I believe that she was changed. Sin entered through her by coming against God's commandment. It made no difference of her "deception." She had broken God's law. In *Genesis 3:6* we read the actual act of the original sin, *"So when the woman saw that the tree was good for food, that it was pleasant to the eyes, and a tree desirable to make one wise, she took of its fruit and ate. She also gave to her husband with her and he ate."* Now, your fate and all humanities were sealed.

Adam had to have seen, known, that she was different. He had to know that the fruit she held in her hand was from the Tree they had been told not to eat from. It is my personal belief that Adam elected, chose of his own free will, to eat that fruit. Why would Adam do so? I believe that his love for Eve, flesh of his flesh, was so strong that he chose to go where ever her course of life would take her. I can hear Adam saying, "Where you go I go." The two had become one.

In that great perfect love, that truly oneness, Adam took her hand to walk together through whatever trials and fate disobedience to God would bring upon them. We have to understand that their becoming one was a lot different than what men and women become today. Theirs was a perfectly created union by God. I can only imagine Adam's love for Eve. A wife created by God for him to love. Perfect in beauty and love for her husband. The joy and happiness they must have shared as they walked through the Garden of Eden. I look forward for the opportunity to ask Adam, his reason, knowing what Eve had done, he chose to eat the forbidden fruit. I look forward to meeting him and so many others in Heaven.

Love is a powerful force. We see the love of a mother for her newborn child, the love a soldier has when he willingly lays down his life for his brothers so they may live. We have seen the great sacrifices many have made for others out of true love or the undying love a husband and wife have shown each other all the days of their lives. Yes, the two can still become one flesh, but only when they both surrender their hearts first to God and then to each other in union blessed by God through the power of the Holy Spirit.

You and I, however, are much different from Adam and Eve. They were a direct creation of God. You and I are descendants of Adam and Eve after they sinned. Born into sin, a fallen race of humanity in need of redemption. They were made perfect – we were not. You and I are the outcome of Adam and Eve's choice to disobey God. Born to have a war within our souls, our empty hearts that long to be filled with either the "will" of God or Satan. There is a day coming when we will be transformed into the perfection God intended for us but yet to be achieved.

Satan, the lord of darkness, has now struck a blow against God and His creation. Satan has taken possession of the "Title Deed" to this Earth. He has now become the ruler of this Earth. There are two reasons we know this to be true. First, we read in *Matthew Chapter 4* the temptation of Jesus Christ by Satan himself. In *Verse 8-10*, we read, *"Again, the devil took Him up on an exceedingly high mountain, and showed Him all the kingdoms of the world and their glory. And he said to Him, "All these things I will give You if You will fall down and worship me." Then Jesus said to him, "Away with you, Satan! For it is written, You shall worship the Lord your God, and Him only you shall serve.""*

Jesus never told Satan he had no power to give Him the kingdoms of this Earth. The reason was because Satan did in fact have the power to do so. There was no challenge by Jesus to his authority or right to offer such a gift. They were Satan's to give. Secondly, we look at the Book of Revelation. Jesus has a scroll. *Revelation 5:1, "And I saw in the right hand of Him who sat on the throne a scroll written inside and on the back, sealed with seven seals."* These are seals which Jesus, and only Jesus, is able to remove.

In the old Jewish custom, when a man borrowed from another a deed, a written document or scroll was created. It was written on the inside with what was required for full payment and redemption. It was sealed with the owners own seal. On the outside of the document was written what a family member needed to do in order to redeem the document and pay the debt in full. Accordingly, as to Jewish custom, a "Goel" or "kinsman redeemer" can repay the debt. In the Hebrew and rabbinical traditions it is a person, the nearest relative that has the "right" to restore all rights and debts. As we will see in following chapters Jesus was the only one who could accomplish this. THE ONLY ONE! Jesus redeemed this document of debt when He died on the cross and rose three days later from the grave. He satisfied our debt which, according to the conditions written on the outside and inside of this scroll, a legal binding document, we would never be able to pay by ourselves. You and I, no matter how holy we believe we are, could never meet the requirements written for redemption. The war started by Satan and allowed to move forward by Adam's sin now had been granted the means of redemption and salvation for the human race.

So, now comes the question of why did all of this have to take place in the first place? That is what this book is all about. *The mystery of one Tree, placed in the Garden of Eden by the Father and the Son.* This is what God has filled in my heart to share with all of you who read this book. There are some of you who will not accept my premise. Some may even curse God for all the pain and suffering this world has endured. The heartfelt pain individually we have lived through and question what kind of God would allow this. But in the end, as you pray for the Lord to reveal the truth, I trust you will see God's wisdom, His sacrifice, His love, and His desired outcome for all of us. Remember as you read, nothing is free. There is always a price that must be paid in one form or another. Can you buy a home without money? No, you cannot. You must work or have some rich family member to pay for it, regardless of how, there is always an exchange of something for another. We learn in our lives there is always a price that must be paid to succeed in our desired goals. The hard work and sweat, the aches and pains, we go through to obtain the simple things in life we desire like a home or car. *To see your son become a man, a husband, a father you are proud of.* It just doesn't happen – it is work and sacrifice. *1 Corinthians 7:23* says, *"You were bought at a price; do not become slaves of men."* Similar is with our Father's plan for you and me.

Chapter 4 – God's Plan

I want to share with you verses from the Bible that show the Father had a plan. This plan also would be implemented and carried out by His Son. The "mystery" of God's plan was held from all those who loved God prior to the revelation of Saul who became Paul in his letter to the Ephesians.

Jesus chose Saul as the one who would write most of the New Testament. The selection of Saul had a lot to do with whom his teacher was. His teacher was a man named Gamaliel. A leader of the Jewish Sanhedrin, a tribunal of appointed "rabbis" to deal with religious, civil and criminal issues in Israel. Gamaliel was a "Pharisee" as was his student, Saul. What better person for Jesus to select than Saul. His understanding of The Old Testament was great. He was a Jew but also a Roman by birth. He was the perfect student for Jesus to select and now, teach and reveal the full measure of truth to Jew and Gentile. In *Galatians Chapter 1* Paul confirms this in *Verse 14, "And I advanced in Judaism beyond many of my contemporaries in my own nation, being more exceedingly zealous for the traditions of my fathers."* We also learn that Paul's new understanding did not come from man, but from Jesus. *Galatians 1:12, "For I neither received it from man, nor was I taught it, but it came through the revelation of Jesus Christ."* You will also find in *Galatians Chapter 1* that Paul took three years for himself to be with Jesus before he went to Jerusalem to see Peter. I remember reading about Jesus, after He rose from the tomb, met disciples on the road to Emmaus, and taught them using the The Old Testament scriptures which spoke of Him. I am sure His conversations with Paul had to be very enlightening.

At this point I would like you all to read Ephesians Chapter 3 in entirety. Now, I want you to read again Verses 3 and 4. This "mystery" spoken of by Paul is "the mystery of Christ." That Christ would come as both man and God, die on a cross and the "church" would be born. That Gentiles would be "heirs" (Verse 6). This wisdom and understanding had been hidden prior until now as we see in *Verse 5*, from all humanity until now. As we read *Verses 9 – 12*, *"and to make all see what is the fellowship of the mystery, which from the beginning of the ages has been hidden in God who created all things through Jesus Christ; to the intent that now the manifold wisdom of God might be made known by the church to the principalities and powers in the heavenly places, according to the eternal purpose which He accomplished in Christ Jesus our Lord, in whom we have boldness and access with confidence through faith in Him."* 1 Peter 1:12 shows us that even the angels in Heaven, serving the Father and the Son, seek to marvel at us. To understand us better, *"…things which angels desire to look into."*

The Father is now revealing to the whole world and *"principalities, and powers in heavenly places,"* His Plan, His Goal, and His Desire as the final outcome of all that has been going on for thousands of years and would now be revealed.

In *Ephesians 1:17-21* we see, *"that the God of our Lord Jesus Christ, the Father of glory, may give to you the spirit of wisdom and revelation in the knowledge of Him, the eyes of your understanding being enlightened; that you may know what is the hope of His calling, what are the riches of the glory of His inheritance in the saints, and what is the exceeding greatness of His power toward us who believe, according to the working of His mighty power which He worked in Christ when He raised Him from the dead and seated Him at His right hand in the heavenly places, far above all principality and power and might and dominion, and every name that is named, not only in this age but also in that which is to come."* The Father is revealing to Paul the truth of His plan. It was the plan of the Father all along. We are the Father's inheritance and through the faithfulness of Jesus, Sons and Daughters of the Most High God and His Son. Reading Ephesians Chapter 1, reveals several interesting facts. First, in Verse 4, we see that the Father chose us before the Earth was created. In Verse 14 we find that we were all "purchased" by Jesus through His sacrifice on the cross. His Son, Jesus, or in Hebrew, "Yeshua", was accordingly in *1 Peter 1:20, "He indeed was foreordained before the foundation of the world, but was manifest in these last times for you."* Yes, before the Earth was formed, before Lucifer, now Satan, and one third of the angels in Heaven were cast out of Heaven to Earth, Jesus knew His fate on a cross, made from a tree He created for the salvation and redemption of the human race. The Father had foreseen all the events of Heaven and Earth that we have read about and experienced personally since the beginning of time.

Therefore, if the Father and His Son knew all that would take place since the beginning of creation, that Lucifer would fall with heavenly angels, then why?

There are two things we need to understand: Why has God allowed this to all move forward and secondly, to reap the "true" harvest of His fruit?

The easy part to understand is what God gets in the end after all is said and done. After a New Heaven and Earth have been created, God's plan for redemption will be complete. You and I will be with our Lord Jesus Christ for all eternity. Will the sacrifices we make on this Earth be worth it? – Yes! Many times over. But the cost to get there, readers, is not always the easiest part to understand or its need. Yes, there is a need for us to reach of our own "free will" the total understanding of the Father's love, and the fullness of that love, in order for this all to come to an end. Ask the Father and Son, through the power of the Holy Spirit, to grant you understanding and wisdom. In Ephesians Chapter 3 we learned of a fellowship of mystery, hidden from previous ages of human history, and made known through the "church", whose eternal purpose was accomplished by the Father through His Son Jesus Christ. That intent and purpose is found in *Ephesians 3:16-19*, *"that He would grant you, according to the riches of His glory, to be strengthened with might through His Spirit in the inner man, that Christ may dwell in your hearts through faith; that you, being rooted and grounded in love, may be able to comprehend with all the saints what is the width and length and depth and height --- to know the love of Christ which passes knowledge; that you may be filled with all the fullness of God."* We will be filled with the fullness of God. We will understand the love of Jesus for every one of us. To be willing to live as one of us and then pay the final price for our freedom from sin and Satan's world of pain and evil. In *Matthew 26* Jesus tells His disciples in *Verse 2*, *"You know that after two days is the Passover, and the Son of Man will be delivered up to be crucified."* To know, beforehand, 11 disciples would abandon Him, one disciple betray Him, face the cruelty of Roman soldiers ripping His flesh from His body, the order of death sealed by a nation He loved, and at the end asking for their forgiveness! What kind of love is that?

Chapter 5 – God's Harvest and Reward

The first thing we must look at is who is the creator of the Earth? We have shown that it was Jesus through the power given to Him by the Father. Jesus is the "rightful landowner," and by such, has the power and the right to harvest the "fruit" of His labor. The next question is, what is the "fruit" of His labor? The answer is simple --you and me. But the next question is, did Jesus have the right to harvest His Church and all the believers since the beginning of time? Well, one can say God can do anything and that is true. But as Paul learned, God says to us "yes," "no" or "not yet" and the Father's reasons are not always known to us. I believe that Jesus HAD to come to Earth to die on a cross, start the greatest revival since the history of time and rightfully claim us as His own. We have shown that before the Earth was formed Jesus knew His fate. What He had to do and what He MUST do. Why? Because of what Adam did and because of who and what we are. Adam was a "direct" creation of God. He walked with God in the cool of the day. But Adam sinned. He and Eve knew they were naked because that was one of the effects to their, now fleshly, bodies. Every human, male or female, since Adam and Eve, has been born through and from sinful bodies. We were born into sin. You and I had no choice but to be born from the sinful mothers we all came from. The Bible teaches us that all have sinned. No man or woman has ever achieved perfection in this life to save themselves or us from sin.

I would venture to say that in the redemption terms of the title deed to Earth there are requirements that a "man of this

Earth" must be the one to redeem it. Jesus is called "The Son of Man." He, of course, is also "The Son of God." You and I, nor even Adam, ever could have met the requirements of redemption and thereby salvation of the human race. Jesus was willing to leave Heaven and pay a price none of us could ever pay. He had to leave Heaven to become one of us, to forever bear the signs of the cross on His body for all eternity and become Man and God all in one. He, Jesus, was the only one who could meet the terms written thousands of years ago for salvation to come to you and me. *Matthew 27:46* is Jesus cry to His Father, *"Eli, Eli, lama sabachthani?", that is, "My God, My God, why have You forsaken Me?"* On the cross His Father had to abandon Him, turn His back on His Son and let Him pay the full painful price of all human sin. Many have said the sacrifice on the cross was the greatest love story. Truer words have never been spoken. It was and always has been about the love of the Father and Son that They have for us. When you finally come to that full realization it will be like being hit with a two-ton truck! It's like seeing on TV a beautiful valley, green hills, heather flowing over them, beautiful birds flying so gracefully and the sun's rays shining over it all. It is another understanding to actually BE THERE! So, it is with the knowledge of our Father's love for each of us. It is powerful, amazing, magical and totally beyond human words. It is the greatest understanding you will ever know.

So, we now see that the Father's plan allowed Satan and his angels to be cast to our Earth where sin entered into all of us from the beginning of time. And because of that, only His Son, the creator of all living things, now being forced to live among us, could save us. I also want to point out another aspect of Jesus as Man.

Jesus used Paul, to bring the gospel to the Gentiles. Jesus was a Jew and as we saw His time was spent with the Jews. I am sure through His travels and teaching there were Gentiles present, but His focus was to the Jews. But after the cross it was opened up to ALL. Jew and Gentile alike, all are considered Sons and Daughters of the Most High God.

If we look at the genealogy of Jesus, we will find interesting people in His bloodline. Through His earthly father, Joseph, we find two names, Ruth and Rahab. Ruth was from the land of Moab and not a Jew. The people of Moab did worship idols. Rahab was in fact a reformed prostitute who let the spies down the back wall of Jericho when Israel came into the promised land. She was the Great-great- great-grandmother to King David! We also see in Mary's genealogy that the son of Boaz and Ruth was Obed the grandfather of King David. Jesus had Gentile blood in His genealogy which gave Him the right to extend His hand to all of us, not just Jews. We see the Father's "hand" in everything to allow His specific outcome.

In *Romans 11:16-21* we read, *"For if the first fruit is holy, the lump is also holy; and if the root is holy, so are the branches. And if some of the branches were broken off, and you, being a wild olive tree, were grafted in among them, and with them became a partaker of the root and fatness of the olive tree, do not boast against the branches. But if you do boast, remember that you do not support the root, but the root supports you. You will say then, "Branches were broken off that I might be grafted in." Well said.*

Because of unbelief they were broken off, and you stand by faith. Do not be haughty, but fear. For if God did not spare the natural branches, He may not spare you either." Some Jews were cut off and we, being Gentiles, were grafted in. After being rejected by Israel, Jesus opened the door to all. So, what is the Father's "outcome?" If we read the words of Jesus in *Matthew 13*, we find part of the answer. Read the whole chapter. Then focus on *Verses 35* through *51*. First, we are the *"good seed"* and those who reject the call of Jesus are the *"tares."* He also tells His disciples that *"the field is the world."* When the trumpet sounds and we who are alive or in a grave will be caught up with Him. We are His prize, the "fruit" spoken of in the Bible. Jesus also said in Verse 35 that He would tell us things kept secret from the foundation of the world. Jesus also tells us what will happen to all those who rejected Him and His reward for faithfulness. *Matthew 13:49 – 50* is very specific, *"So it will be at the end of the age. The angels will come forth, separate the wicked from among the just, and cast them into the furnace of fire. There will be wailing and gnashing of teeth."* I would also like you to read *Romans 9:18-24*. The Father will show mercy on those whom He wills, He is the potter and you and I are His clay. Through our own individual "free will" and the ingrained understanding of good and evil given to us through one tree by Adam and Eve, we elect to love the Father and His Son, or to follow Satan and the false desires he will place upon the hearts of those who follow him. We read in *Romans 8:28*, *"And we know that all things work together for good to those who love God, to those who are the called according to His purpose."* We are all called according to the Father's purpose. But, not all answer the call. Therefore, the fate of many will lead them into an eternal separation from the Father and Son because they freely choose to reject God's desire for their lives.

All through the Bible we see the Father's hand in everything: from Moses, who wrote the first books of the Bible and brought Israel out of Egypt, through all the specific events and trials that led to the creation of Israel. Noah and only his family were saved out of all humanity to foil Satan. Today we witness, the shortening of the human life span, and the confusion of human language. The miracle of the Bible is a complete message and instruction from the Father which is available to the whole world. We see God's hand, and those actions of His Son, that have brought us to where we are today. Just as the ruler of Babylon, Belshazzar saw an angel write on a wall his fate and the kingdom's, so we see the hand writing on the wall of Earth. We see the leaves changing color and know that the time of the Lord is coming very soon. The Plan is about to be finished. We see wars and rumors of wars, the decline of moral values, the cheapness of human life as in little babies chopped up and sold like so much meat, and leaders looking to remove the freedoms we have shed so much blood for to rule over us like simple sheep. In all of this, I always had one last question – why so long and so much human suffering? My answer to that is what the next chapter is all about. I once said that all things have a price. Nothing is really free. Somewhere, somehow, someone has paid the price, and if someone is willing to pay the price, therefore, the reward must be worth it. Especially if the price has been very heavy. Let's look at the next question in our next chapter.

Chapter 6 – Why the Cost

I recently knew a young girl who became very sick. She was not a Christian. She knew who Jesus was but had no relationship with him. She was afraid because the specialist who was treating her told her this could be life and death. She reached out to her grandmother in tears because she was afraid of dying. Her grandmother did have a relationship with Jesus. She wanted prayer, she wanted Jesus to help her and she needed to know how to reach Him. Isn't this true of all of us at one time or another? We never think of Jesus until we are faced with a dire turn of events.

When Adam sinned, and from the womb of Eve all humanity came into existence, we have had "the knowledge of good and evil" in our very DNA. You never have to teach a child how to be bad. Ask any parent. We have to learn how to be good. How to act, dress, speak, use proper words, the meaning of respect of others, and honor. One tree in the Garden of Eden imparted to everyone the total knowledge of good and evil. We watch TV and instantly know what is good or bad. We know what actions are good or bad. What we should see or run away from. We instinctively "know" this! You've heard the expression, "you know that you know." That is because we all do. When the Father and His Son placed the Tree of the Knowledge of Good and Evil in the garden for Satan to use, it caused sin to enter into this world. They knew what They were doing and what the result would be.

You and I are born with "free will." We get to choose how to live our lives the way we want to. Yes, there are governments that try to rule over us against our will. In the end, however, we elect to make a choice of our own free will. It comes down to what has been said for thousands of years, *"whom will you serve."* There are two choices. Jesus our King and His Father or Satan and his angels. So why has God allowed all the human suffering in order to reap His reward?

I want you to consider a true Samurai Sword. The process of folding the metal to create such a sword is called "shita-kitae." The steel is heated and pounded by hand and folded over 1,000 times to remove the impurities. A master by the name of Honjo Masamune created one of the earliest and one of the finest ever made. I can only imagine what one would sell for today. In 1992 Dr. Walter Ames Compton sold one Kamakura from the 13th Century for $418,000.

This Earth is God's furnace. Here we are heated by trials, hammered, folded and beaten again to remove the filth of the world from our "hearts." Look at Moses, it took God 40 years to topple Pharaoh's tyranny through him. Look at what so many Christians have had to go through before they surrendered their hearts to God. The purpose of this testing is to see what our hearts are made of and how God can change them. We know that God is Love. If He was a hard cold master none of us would be alive today. He looks at our lives before we were ever born and knowing, if in the end of our days, we will love Him of our own free will. I don't mean just know of Him, but love Him. I did not come to truly being saved until I realized what the "love of God," the true "love of Jesus" was in its fullest measure. Or at least as a human is capable of. We read about it, acknowledge it, but few feel it. It resides in only one place – the heart. The word "heart" is used 826 times in the Bible. If you would take the time to read each word, used in its full context, you would find an interesting discovery. A realization, an understanding you will find that touches your heart in a way as never before. This is what the harvest is all about. Those who truly love the Lord, know Him personally, have a relationship with Him, talk with Him, pray, and Honor Him and the Father. It is a daily time invested relationship, fellowship and love. You can't reach there by walking into church once a week or on Easter while continue living in the world the rest of the week. How does a father or mother know their children, really? They spend time with them, go on trips with them and are an integral part of their daily lives. So, it must be with our Lord if we are to become His children.

God created Adam and Eve. He created angels. He did not create sinful bodies that hate, that knowingly and willfully abuse children. We are the direct result of sin but through God's grace and mercy, His love, and His desire to have us love Him, worship Him and His Son of our own free will, we come to love Them. We don't love Him because He wrote a bunch of laws on stone tablets. No! Christians live their lives because they LOVE God. We don't do what the rest of the world does out of fear. Fear and love can never exist in the same room, neither can fear shroud our lives. Does the Bible say to "fear God?" Yes, it does. When you come to the full realization of what He can do, yes, you should fear Him. Bear in mind that is not what He truly wants. He wants you and me to love Him and His Son because of Their love for us.

Chapter 7 - The Failure of Israel

Israel is the greatest example of the inability of fear and laws to ever be the means by which a human will leave the lusts of this world and follow God. David wrote in the *Psalms 81:12, "So I gave them over to their own stubborn heart, To walk in their own counsels."* Israel could have been that shining light upon a hill, a light to the whole world that following the God of Israel would bring favor, rewards, joy, happiness and peace.

As we read in the Bible, God chose Abraham to be the father of the Jewish Nation – Israel. God brought them into Egypt to thrive and become a separate people. As time passed the nation grew in numbers. We see that the new leadership of Egypt no longer remembered what had been done to save their nation and make them prosper. God allowed His people to come under the rule of Egypt and to suffer through the persecution of Egypt until a man named Moses returned to liberate them.

God showed the people that He is their one true God. That His power and abilities would unshackle them via miracles that would make humans today shudder in fear. God showed, through Egypt, His might and power. Those events and the fall of Jericho set fear into all the people of the promised land that would one day become the Kingdom of Israel. In *2 Kings 19:35* we read, *"And it came to pass on a certain night that the angel of the Lord went out, and killed in the camp of the Assyrians one hundred and eighty-five thousand; and when the people arouse early in the morning there were the corpses – all dead.*" God has legions of angels, yet it took only one to extinguish the threat and fear of Israel's enemy. As you study the Bible you will find numerous examples of God's interventions on behalf of Israel. For hundreds of years He watched over Israel, chastised them, and forgave them.

It has been estimated that in the 6th Century BC that the population of Israel was around 800,000 people. We find that Israel had fallen into Idol worship. They worshiped a god called Baal. In *1 Kings 19:18* we read, *"Yet I have reserved seven thousand in Israel, all whose knees have not bowed to Baal, and every mouth that has not kissed him."* Only seven thousand out of so many. After all that the Lord had shown, done for the nation, only a few were faithful. Why were the people so easy to fall astray? I would encourage you to read of the journey of Israelites from the time they left Egypt until they actually entered into the promised land. You will find, time and time again, stories of their rejection of God and Moses. In the book of Numbers chapter 16 you will find the story of Korah, Dathan, and Abiram. Because of their rejection of the Lord and His servant Moses, God carved the Earth where they stood and swallowed them and all their belongings. More were to perish as you finish the chapter for their lack of faith and trust in God. What I find amazing, is that after Israelites had seen God perform through His display of power and justice, these peoples still stood ready to defy God and come against His servant, Moses. A trait we will see throughout hundreds of years of their existence.

The people of Israel had "hardened their hearts" to the point of total blindness. In *Hebrews 3:7–19*, we find the answer to the fall of Israel. As you read these verses you find the truth of their nature and their heart. Their utter refusal to believe. This same trait that condemned thousands of Jews to die in the desert sands, and never enter the promised land, continued throughout their history. Read all the verses in Hebrews chapter 3. Look at *Verse 15, "Today, if you will hear His voice, Do not harden your hearts as in rebellion."* A verse written so many years ago, yet as it says, "Today" still applies in our time and time to come if we will only listen.

Jesus told his disciples in *Matthew 13:15, "For the hearts of this people have grown dull."* Jesus pronounced seven woes to the religious leaders of Israel in *Matthew 23:13-36.* They were condemned for their hypocrisy and blindness. Jesus finally told the people there would be no more signs but one. In *Matthew 16:4* we read, *"A wicked and adulterous generation seeks after a sign, and no sign shall be given to it except the sign of the Prophet Jonah."* That would be Him rising from His tomb. The nation and its people had seen signs for hundreds of years. Yet, they would not believe. In Israel's own selfish and cold heart they took the Son of God, the Son of Man, and killed Him in cold blood. They did so with intent and purpose of heart.

What do we learn from the nation of Israel? That the power of sin is so strong, so perverse, and if left to run unopposed it would destroy all mankind and every living thing on this Earth. Our Creator, Jesus, came to the Earth as one of us. He came to His chosen people, the Nation of Israel. For hundreds of years, He had been patient with His people, forgiven their sins, protected them, blessed them beyond all other peoples. Imagine for a moment what the world would be like IF Israel had obeyed God. How different life would be and how you would have reacted to seeing a nation so blessed and protected by the one true God. However, Satan and his virus called sin infected the nation to its core. It was no longer possible for them to be the hope of this world, an example of obeying God that would reveal a much better life than anything Satan could offer. Now the door to becoming Sons and Daughters of the Most High God would be open to all human life. All that was required was to have faith in His Son – Jesus – and follow Him with all your heart.

Chapter 8-The Heart

We live in a proving ground called Earth that will test our hearts, our moral character and fiber. It will test our very being and every moment of our lives. There is a real force seeking to dominate the very heart, the spiritual force that lives within you and me.

What did God say in *Genesis 6:5-6, "Then the Lord saw that the wickedness of man was great in the Earth, and that every intent of the thoughts of his heart was only evil continually. And the Lord was sorry that He had made man on the earth, and He was grieved in His heart."* God is looking at your heart. From your heart comes thoughts, from thoughts come desires, and from your desires come your actions. It starts in the heart, and not in your brain. Good and evil are determined in the heart. We also see that the Father and the Son actually have a heart too. Without the love of Their hearts towards you and me, we all would be dead.

King David, called a "man after God's own heart" wrote in *Psalms 78:38-39, "But He, being full of compassion, forgave their iniquity, And did not destroy them. Yes, many a time He turned His anger away, And did not stir up all His wrath; For He remembered that they were but flesh, A breath that passes away and does not come again."* I contemplate how many times Jesus should have taken away my life for my sins. It is so true that this flesh, in which our spirits dwell, will never see Heaven. When we die, we will never have to live in this flesh ever again. I take joy in that beyond measure. Not because I will not have to watch my diet or other habits of self-indulgence, but I will never, for all eternity, have to deal with the effects of sin upon myself or those whom I love, who elect to make Jesus their Lord and Savior.

In Strongs Exhaustive Concordance of the Bible the word "heart" is mentioned 826 times. The heart is the focus of the physical and spiritual being. *Isaiah 14:12-17* tells us it was Lucifer's "heart" that allowed his pride and jealousy to sin. *1 Samuel 16:7* tells us that man looks at the physical appearance but God looks at the heart. *1 Corinthians 4:5, "Therefore judge nothing before the time, until Lord comes, who will both bring to light the hidden things of darkness and reveal the counsels of the hearts..."* This shows us that God will reveal the counsels of our heart. We believe that we can hide our bad behavior from family and this world. Our honest mistakes, maybe, but the sinful deeds of our lives will one day be exposed for all to see. The true nature of our hearts will be revealed and the righteousness of God and His Son will be understood when judgment of our lives comes.

The Father and the Son want to have Sons and Daughters who, of their own free will, not out of fear or law books, elect to love Them because we have felt in totality Their love for us. I was once asked about my experience in Vietnam during my tour in 1968 and 1969 with the 173rd Airborne. I fought with men possessing great courage and honor and watched men die next to me. Men who were willing to die so the rest of us could live. I was asked if I still "loved them?" I said, "how could I not after all they gave for me." I was then asked, what about the love that Jesus had for all of us, to go through the horror of the cross? I realized, for the first time in my life, the depth of His love for me. If He, God, living in

Heaven, was willing to be forever changed, to live as one of us, grow up as a boy, a man, and go through the sufferings of rejection from those He made and physically endure the cross – well, how could I NOT love Him?

True love comes naturally from the heart. It cannot be taught in school books. We use that word in our world so casually that it loses all meaning, but true love comes from the heart. When a mother looks into the eyes of her just born baby for the first time her heart overwhelms with love. Or the love of a father when he sees his son raising his own family in the Lord. Love comes from the heart. All evil comes from the heart. God wants our hearts. The sad part is we have to go through the trial by fire, the hammering of our hearts, the continuous folding and beating that purifies our hearts until we finally understand God's love, Jesus's love for us and we submit.

Paul, Peter, Timothy, James all called themselves "bondservants." In *Exodus 21*, Moses tells us what that term truly means. That your love for your master is so great, that his kindness, his treatment of you and those you love, is so strong, that you, of your own free will, elect to serve him all the days of your life with joy and happiness. To know Christ is to love Him, and to love Him with all your heart is to serve Him with joy throughout all eternity. Why do the angels marvel at us? They see all that humanity has and still is going through in order to come to the Lord.

There is a price we all must be willingly to pay. The words we use in conversations, the movies we watch, the way we live our lives each day must be in line with the principles

Jesus taught us during His time with us. At the time of the harvest, Jesus will be called to come and take those who belong to Him up into Heaven for our rewards for faithfulness, even unto death. I marvel at the courage of the Christian families who face persecution and death every day. They refuse to deny Christ even though they know their fate could be sealed for believing in Jesus Christ. Their love for Jesus is that strong, and that firm.

As I stated, the Bible mentions the "heart" 826 times. God is telling us that our heart is the most important part of our body; greater than the mind or any other part. Everything stems from the heart. *1 Samuel 16:7, "...For the Lord does not see as man sees; for man looks at the outward appearance, but the Lord looks at the heart." 1 Chronicles 28:9, "As for you, my son Solomon, know the God of your father, and serve Him with a loyal heart and with a willing mind; for the Lord searches all hearts and understands all the intent of the thoughts. If you seek Him, He will be found by you; but if you forsake Him, He will cast you off forever." Proverbs 16:9, "A man's heart plans his way, But the Lord directs his steps." In Proverbs 17:3 we read, "The refining pot is for silver and the furnace for gold, But The Lord tests the hearts."* This world is God's furnace where all the impurities of our lives are removed until we, of our free will, turn our hearts over to Him. We are the Father's golden treasure and soon the Father is going to tell His Son it is time for the Harvest. I want you to listen to what Jeremiah reveals to us in *Chapter 17:9-10, "The heart is deceitful above all things, And desperately wicked; Who can know it? I, the Lord, search the heart, I test the mind, Even to give every man according to his ways, According to the fruit of his doings."* We see from these verses, and so many more, that God looks to the "heart," to understand our intents, and thereby our purpose and actions in our lives. Are they for Him, and His will? Or, are they for our selfish nature and Satan's?

I strongly encourage each reader to take the time, as a matter of study, to go through all 826 verses that deal with the heart. I believe you will come away a much different person than when you started. I have never regretted the time it took to read them, or the time of deep contemplation through which the Holy Spirit molded me. That is not to say I have no more room for growth. I will grow in the Lord all the days of my life until my last breath is taken and my spirit returns from whence it came. For thousands of years it has been and always will be about the HEART.

One simple, yet profound, example of God's reason for putting the Tree of The Knowledge of Good and Evil in the Garden is found in the Book of *Romans 1:20*. Paul said, *"For since the creation of the world His invisible attributes are clearly seen, being understood by the things that are made, even His eternal power and Godhead, so that they are without excuse."* That is because we all have the internal God given knowledge of both good and evil. We will never be able to stand before God and say, "I didn't know." On December 17th, 2004, I wrote a note to myself, "Will, not feelings determines moral direction. Sin is corruption of will. The will is governor of the heart." Our God given "free will" allows each of us to choose a path for all eternity. Ask yourself, what path am I on? Which road and its final destination am I on?

We know God has a time limit. Thank God. We know that when the fullness of the Gentiles comes in, the Antichrist will be revealed. That means the book of Revelation will be opened and the very end is near. There is one final trial, one final example of why sin can never be allowed to exist

Chapter 9-Jesus Returns as King

After we return with Christ to establish His Kingdom on Earth for a thousand years, the final trial of good verses evil will begin. We know that not all human life will perish during the Tribulation described in the Book of Revelation. There will be some left alive to experience a new life under the True King – Jesus Christ. In the Book of *Zechariah, Chapter 14* we see the conclusion of the war against Israel and its outcome. *Verse 17* of the chapter says, *"And it shall be that whichever of the families of the earth do not come up to Jerusalem to worship the King, the Lord of hosts, on them there will be no rain."* So why is God giving some humans another chance of eternal life? Satan has had thousands of years to flaunt his intentions for you and me. The type of ruler he would be and the type of world he would rule over. Now, the time has come for Jesus and His Father to show the type of world, under Their rule, the Earth would be like.

Imagine living in our world where the lion and lamb play together. No sickness, no wars, nothing or no one will try to kill us. No one will steal, rape or murder. There will be no need for cable nor Internet. Children will be able to live without the fears of this life they face. Mothers will not have to worry someone will kidnap their children for the wicked desires sin has poured in their evil hearts. Life will be simpler but full. We won't need locks on our doors. I venture to say that those who feel they want to try to go back to their sinful lives will find that path closed. For a thousand years life will be free and full of peace and happiness.

In the end, as described in *Revelation 20:7-10*, Satan will receive his final opportunity to come against Jesus and the Saints. Satan will deceive, convince humans to revolt against those who believe in Jesus. One final battle will take place and the final end will come to Satan, his angels, and those whose hearts are turned against Jesus and the Father. Their end will be swift and final. God's plan for our Earth and the human race will be finished. The final revelation of the effects of sin, even in the face of a life under the King, will be revealed. There will be no doubt that sin can never be allowed to exist. Paul said in *Galatians 5:9, "A little leaven leavens the whole lump."* Meaning, that even a little sin will ruin the whole world, all life and bring about death and destruction. Everyone's fate will be sealed. Their "free will," given to each of us, will determine our hearts choice of whom we will serve. It is hard to believe that a person would elect to live in their old sick ways rather than walking in beautiful fields of green and color. Imagine a world where human and lion, predator and prey, sit together, a world devoid of illness and fear. Just Imagine!

The Conclusion

A new Heaven and Earth will be born. There we will worship the King and His Father. We will serve Them according to Their will in our lives and we will never have one regret of the choice we have made. The joy and happiness we will experience will be beyond anything we can imagine. We will be true Sons and Daughters of the Most High God for all Eternity. They will have us, who love Them, of our own free will, who have endured the trials of Earth that marvel even the angels.

What did the Father accomplish with His Plan? First, Satan and his angels were removed from Heaven. The nature of sin, as shown through thousands of years of human existence, was revealed through the desires of Satan and his angels. That revelation is utter destruction, pain, suffering, and finally death. Second, the Father now has a race of unique humans. They, of their own free will, given the choice of the desires Satan offered or the promises offered by giving your heart to Jesus as your King, chose Jesus. Not out of fear, beautiful things, gold or silver, but out of true love. We have become bondservants of our own free will to a King worthy of our devotion and loyalty. We, born into sinful flesh, given free will, elected to love Them! No one pointed a gun to our heads and said love God or else. We walked into this love relationship freely.

Was it worth it? Yes, it was. Was the price too high? The Son, Jesus, will forever bear the signs in His body of the price He paid and His willingness to do so. Prior to coming to this Earth, Jesus never had a heavenly body that showed the signs in His feet, hands, and His side for all eternity as a remembrance of His sacrifice and love for us. You and I, in our new forms of life, shall forever have within us the knowledge of good and evil. We will be the ones who lived through the fire of trials upon an Earth we were born into. That wisdom will always be with us in a special, unique way that not even the angels will have. We shall forever be the children of Father, Son and Spirit. There was never in Heaven a race of humans such as we will be. Before Adam and Eve, all were created beings. We were born through the trials of this earthly life and experienced, in real painful terms, the nature of sin. We lived under the rule of Satan until Jesus paid the price and broke our sinful chains. Never in Heaven, according to what we read in the Bible, was there ever such a race of beings as what we shall become. We will be unique in Heaven. The wisdom, the understanding of the true nature of sin, imparted to us through the one tree, The Tree of the Knowledge of Good and Evil, lived through and experienced in living terms on Earth, will be with us for all eternity. To the Father's glory and purpose, we shall be what He, and His Son, desired thousands of years ago – heavenly beings who love them out of "free will." Something never seen in Heaven until that day comes when we go home. Was the price heavy? Yes it was very heavy, sad, painful, yet according to the Father's plan worth it and necessary to reap the harvest of His desire. Do we all have regrets? Yes, we all do. Do I wish I had been smarter, wiser in my youth – without a doubt! Learn from the past and move into the future. Today I am free, with the knowledge of my destiny, and no longer bound by the chains of a sinful life.

Ah, but there is still, though, one more plan for all of us and for each individual. We are told that we will rule and reign with our King, that we will judge angels. To what end and to what purpose? I ask. That is the next great mystery to be revealed! Whatever it is, I have no doubt, we will not be disappointed in any way. However, we still have work to finish.

So, what will you do now? How will you live your life today and tomorrow? As Paul said, put on the whole armor of God so you can fend off the arrows of Satan and his angels. Stay the course, fight the good fight and gain redemption. Of your own free will choose Jesus as you King. Surrender your total, complete heart to Him. I promise you one thing. You will never regret it.

May the Lord bless you and keep you. Amen

Made in the USA
Columbia, SC
15 February 2024

31588888R00033